Writing Lessons from the Front: Book 4

Track down the
Weasel Words

*And other strategies to revise and
improve your manuscript*

Angela Hunt

Other Books in the Writing Lessons from the Front Series

The Plot Skeleton, Book 1

Creating Extraordinary Characters, Book 2

Point of View, Book 3

Track Down the Weasel Words, Book 4

Evoking Emotion, Book 5

Write Your Book: Plans and Process, Book 6

Hunt Haven Press

ISBN: 0615844480
ISBN-13: 978-0615844480

"Omit needless words."

--William Strunk Jr., *The Elements of Style*

1 THE ONE AND ONLY CHAPTER

Suppose Joe's car battery dies. He takes it to a mechanic who tells him to come back in an hour. Joe does, and finds the mechanic smiling as he wipes his hands on a towel. "Good to see you," he says. "You'll be happy to know that your bill comes to $2500.00."

Joe gasps. "Twenty-five hundred dollars! What kind of battery did you put in?"

"An ordinary one," the mechanic says. "But I also threw in 250 unnecessary parts."

Makes no sense, does it? Joe doesn't want to pay for parts he doesn't need. And extra parts won't help his car run better. In fact, unnecessary parts will only clunk around under the hood, possibly destroying his engine.

Joe demands that the extra parts be removed, the bill be reduced, and he vows never to visit that mechanic again.

Now let's say Joe writes an article for *Southern Life*. He sends it to the editor, who sends it back post haste. Upset by her rejection of what Joe considered an excellent piece, he breaks every rule of writer's etiquette and calls to ask why she rejected his work.

"I liked your topic," she says, "but your writing was all over the place and I don't have time to rewrite every article that comes in. You used too many words to make one or two points, and I'm not paying for writing that doesn't work."

In short, Joe and his mechanic have the same problem.

Ever since man has been putting pen to paper, the goal of the disciplined writer has been to say as much as possible in as few words as possible. We look for verbs with punch, descriptive nouns, and we scratch out dozens of adverbs and adjectives.

My favorite English teacher, the late Janet Williams, used to tell us that we could pay ourselves a quarter for every word we could

5

cut out of our compositions. Back in those days we were tossing in every word we could think up to fill the required amount of pages, so her advice went against our natural instincts. But for those of us who took writing seriously, her advice proved to be golden.

And over the years, I have amassed a mountain of quarters by heeding her advice. I've been writing professionally for thirty years, publishing over 120 books as well as hundreds of magazine articles. Why? Because along the way I've learned to write tight.

You can, too.

This lesson is a collection of easy-to-remember guidelines, tips, and techniques to help you improve your novel, short story, nonfiction article or book, or term paper. Not every section will apply to your project, but many of them will apply to any kind of writing.

So settle back, grab a marker or pencil, and get ready to revise your manuscript. You'll be amazed at how easy it is to track down the weasel words that eat away at the effectiveness of your writing.

Prologues

If you've written a prologue or introduction to your book or novel, set your emotions aside and look at it with a critical eye. If it

- reveals what you're going to repeat in a later chapter
- steals material from an exciting scene in an effort to hook the reader
- consists of historical backstory to "set the stage"
- adds no real value to the work as a whole,

delete it. And when you delete it, don't just hit the delete key—I know how painful that can be. Instead, create a folder on your computer or in your desk and label it "Cut Materials." By placing cut sections in that folder, you're not annihilating them, you're reserving them in case you need them again.

Which you probably won't.

Why?

If your prologue or introduction only told the reader what you were going to tell him anyway, think of a way you can do that without actually using the same words. Use a quote that echoes the theme. Look for an anecdote to illustrate an important principle of your book or article. Find another way to entice the reader and prepare him without actually repeating the material you're going to use later.

If your work is fiction and your prologue or introduction consisted of an excerpt from an exciting scene near the end of your book, find another interesting way to open your story. You don't have to open with a car chase, a bomb, or a kidnapping, but you do have to arouse the reader's sympathy and interest. How? Have your character do something interesting, and put something at risk if your character fails. The reader will keep reading because he wants to know if your character will succeed in getting out of the house in time for his important job interview.

I don't know how many times I've had the TV on as background noise and I'll inadvertently become interested in some mindless, idiotic show. My husband will call me, and I'll say, "Just a minute. I have to find out if Toni makes it to the prom or not."

Do I really care about Toni and her prom? Not in the least, because they have nothing to do with my real life. But the TV writers have hooked me with the material, I sympathize with Toni, and I want to stick around long enough to see if she makes it to her school dance.

If your prologue or introduction is historical information (in a novel, it's called 'backstory'), you can usually cut it without a second thought. I don't know any faster way to put a reader to sleep than to regale him with historical information. If, however, this information is brief, active, and extremely well-written, you could make a good case for keeping it.

If you cut your prologue or introduction because it adds no real value to the work, put it in the "cut materials" folder and let it rest in peace. You'll earn a pile of quarters for your brave sacrifice.

Your Opening Paragraphs

While we're looking at the beginning of your manuscript, let's take a moment to think like a book buyer. What is the first thing a browsing reader sees that might entice him to pick up your book?

Ten points if you answered "the spine." Unfortunately, we don't have much control over the spine, so there's not much to worry about unless you are also designing your own cover.

So what's the next area that a potential book buyer considers? Right, the front cover. It may be unfortunate, but people *do* judge a book by its cover, so do your best to make sure yours looks good. If you're publishing with a traditional publisher, this, too, might be out of your control, but if you're self-publishing you will need to hire a good graphic artist to design a cover for you. I have made covers for a few of my e-books and, frankly, they looked amateurish. I learned my lesson, and now try to leave cover design to the professionals.

The next thing a potential book buyer looks at? Back cover copy, usually, and though publishers rarely ask for it, I always submit potential back cover copy along with my manuscript. No one at the publishing house knows my book as well as I do, so I figure that I can at least give them some copy to adjust as they try to create an enticing back cover.

Now we're down to factors we control completely: what's the next thing a potential book buyer examines? The first page. He flips past the front matter and reads the first sentence or two, and that's it. Studies have shown that potential buyers spend less than six seconds looking at that first page, and in that six seconds they make up their minds about whether or not to buy the book.

So don't waste your opening line. It may be the most important sentence in your entire manuscript.

Writers have come up with all sorts of memorable openings, from Snoopy's infamous "It was a dark and stormy night" to Melville's "Call me Ishmael."

My personal favorite first line comes from Jodi Picoult's *Second Glance*: "Ross Wakeman succeeded the first time he tried to kill himself, but not the second or the third."[1]

Isn't that delicious? Wouldn't you keep reading? I sure would— and did.

I can't give you a formula for writing a killer first sentence, but I can give you some guidelines. First, avoid weather reports and descriptions of landscapes or furniture. Second, include a person and a provocative question.

That's it. Make sure your first sentence is active, not static, and that someone is doing something.

Whenever I teach fiction classes over several sessions, I always have my students write their first line on a piece of paper and hand it to me. I then read each of those sentences to the class, asking for honest responses: hands up high for "Yes, I'd keep reading," hands slightly raised for "maybe I'd keep reading," and no uplifted hands at all for "it's not working for me."

It's an eye-opening experience when writers see how real people receive their first line.

So spend extra time—as much as you need—on that first line. It's more important than you may realize.

After the First Line

You can't coast after you come up with that killer first sentence. The rest of the first scene must be top-notch, too. You keep a reader reading by withholding information. You tell him what he needs to know, but not a mite more.

The following probably applies more to fiction than nonfiction writers, but the principle is the same: don't dump a lot of details on your nonfiction reader in the beginning. Tell him what he needs to know, but only when he needs to know it.

If, like a lot of beginning novelists, you try to explain everything as you move through the material, you'll do a great job of eradicating all suspense from your book. Memorize this: you don't want to answer all the reader's questions, you want to raise questions in his mind. Think of it as "baiting" the reader. Your job is to toss out little hooks to snag his interest and keep him reading. You can't do that if you've explained everything.

My novel *Magdalene* opens with these paragraphs:

> Silence, as heavy as doom, wraps itself around me as two guards lead me into the lower-level judgment hall. When I fold my hands, the *chink* of my chains disturbs the quiet.
>
> My judge, Flavius Gemellus, senior centurion of the *Cohors Secunda Italica Civum Romanorum*, looks up from the rolls of parchment on his desk, his eyes narrow. I don't blame him for being annoyed. I am not a Roman citizen, so I have no right to a trial. Besides, I have confessed and am ready to die.[2]

When I teach this material in person, I read the above passage and ask my students to quickly lift their hands when I've read something that makes them ask a question. Let's look at these paragraphs again, and I'll mark the places where I usually see a flutter of hands:

> Silence, as heavy as doom, wraps itself around me as two guards lead me into the lower-level judgment hall. *[Where is she?]* When I fold my hands, the *chink* of my chains disturbs the quiet. *[Why is she in chains?]*
>
> My judge, Flavius Gemellus, senior centurion of the *Cohors Secunda Italica Civum Romanorum*, looks up from the rolls of parchment on his desk, his eyes narrow. I don't blame him for being annoyed. I am not a Roman citizen, so I have no right to a trial. *[Why is she on trial?]* Besides, I have confessed and am ready to die. *[Why would anyone confess, and why is she ready to die?]*

Do you see how it's done? As a storyteller, your task is to raise questions in the reader's mind, not to reveal everything up front. Editors will often write RUE in the margins of a manuscript—the letters stand for *resist the urge to explain*. Respect your reader's intelligence enough to let them figure things out, and don't reveal anything the reader doesn't absolutely need to know.

One note: Hooking the reader is not the same thing as leaving your reader in confusion. The reader isn't confused after reading the above passage; he's only asking questions. If the reader is confused because your writing makes no sense, he's likely to put your work down and not pick it up again.

Backstory—anything in a novel or short story that happens before the present story time—should be reserved for the back of the story. Too many beginning writers start out with something vital and interesting, but in chapter two they give us what I call the "backstory dump," which tells us about everything that occurred between the time Grandpa arrived in this country to when Papa died last year. The reader doesn't need to know all of that in chapter two, if they need to know it at all. So put all of it in your "cut materials" file, and later, when you need your protagonist to reflect on an emotional moment from the past, pull out that brief snippet about Papa dying and flesh it out into a scene. Let us see Papa propped up on his pillows, his face pale and sunken; let our heroine feel his callused hand as she grasps it. Then let him whisper words she will never forget.

Do you see? If you change some backstory into flashbacks and use them after we are fully engaged with the character, we will be much more emotionally involved with your characters. And that's our aim.

Now let's move from big picture revisions to some of the little details. From macro to micro.

What are Weasel Words?

They are words that clutter up your manuscript. Some of them are common to almost everyone who speaks English; others are unique to each writer. For instance, after I handed in one book, the editor called and said I was using *pull* too much.

I was flabbergasted. "Pull?"

"Yes," she said. "You have people *pulling* into driveways, *pulling* onto roads, *pulling* things from their purses and pockets. The word is all over the place."

I shook my head. "I didn't realize."

But I went back and did a search for the word *pull* in my manuscript—and there it was, sprinkled like paprika every few paragraphs. I deleted some, changed some to *turned*, others to *took*, others to *tugged*. But now I'm much more aware of my use of the word *pull*.

Tools for Tracking

The best tool for tracking down your weasel words is your word processing program's search and replace feature. If you write in any of the standard programs—Word, Word Perfect, Scrivener, Pages—you will find *search* (or *find*) and *replace*. When you're searching for a particular weasel word, ask your program to search for the word with spaces before and after it (unless it's a word likely to be used several times at the end of a sentence. In that case, you'll want to omit the last space).

For instance, if I was searching for it, I would enter [space]it[space] in the search box. Then I'd enter [space]IT[space] in the *replace* box. If you forget to add the spaces, the program will capitalize every instance of *it* in your book, and you'll have to manually change them back to what they should be.

That's what I do for every weasel word on my list. I use search and replace to find the word or phrase (with spaces), then I replace it with the exact same word or phrase, except in all capital letters (also with spaces before and after). This doesn't change any of my

11

prose, but those weasel words now LOOM on the page and catch my attention as I work through subsequent drafts. And every time I see one, I stop and ask myself if I can make the sentence better without that word. If I can, great. If I can't—or if it would make the sentence too convoluted—the sentence remains as it was.

Identifying the Weasel Words

The first weasel word is one I first noticed the year I taught high school English. I'd never thought of it as a weasel word, but suddenly there it was, all over my students' papers. I grew weary of circling it with my bright red pen, and over and over again I drew little weasel faces in the margins of their papers.

A very small, very overused word. Can you guess what it is?

Yes! IT!

It is so common we really don't think about it, but sometimes we fall into patterns that result in what I call "vague its." This particular species of *it* has infested many a sentence. When you find one of these, the best thing to do is shoot it and start over by asking, "What am I really trying to say here?"

Example: Mary wore a blue dress with flowers on *it*.

Does that *it* cause you to stop or slow down in any way? Can you tell immediately what *it* represents?

Yes, the blue dress. You shouldn't have to think too long about that *it*, so it's a good *it*. You could keep it, though you could earn some quarters by writing:

Mary wore a blue flowered dress.

The *it* that weakens your prose is found in sentences like this:

It is hard to get a drivers' license.

Hmm. What does that first *it* stand for? You have to think a moment, don't you? *It* has no apparent connection to anything else in the sentence, the paragraph, or the world.

So back up and say what you're really trying to say:

Getting a driver's license is hard. Or complicated. Or whatever you really meant.

What about this example:

"You don't understand," Mom said, sniffling. "*It's* so hard to live without your Dad."

In the second example, the questionable *it* is found in dialogue, and we loosen up when considering dialogue because people talk in all kinds of ways. If your character doesn't use proper grammar when she's crying and upset, she's just like the rest of us. Welcome her to the human race, and let her keep her undefined *it*.

Pardoning Reasonable Weasels

Please understand that the principles I'm presenting in this book are not hard and fast rules. I'm not saying all prologues are wrong or every *it* should be condemned or it's always wrong to use italics. Writing is part craft and part art, and I would never want to infringe on anyone's art . . . as long as they knew what they were doing. But when people make a word mess and call it art, well . . . I'm not likely to read it.

Doesn't mean everyone else will feel the same way.

So if you want to write *It's the way he smiled that made me love him*, no one's going to demand that you be tarred and feathered by the writer police.

But as you sit down to revise and edit your manuscript, it's a good idea to search for *[space]it[space]* and replace it with the same term, but in capital letters. Look at each of the *its* you find in your manuscript, and see if each one is clearly related to the word it represents. If so, fine, no problem. But if you have a disturbing number of the noisome vague *its*, perhaps you should consider their eradication.

Passive Verbs

We are a video generation. We have grown up with film and television and instant-everything. We microwave and keep the Internet at our fingertips. We Google for information, we call up maps in our cars, and we can even send emails through our refrigerators.

So why wouldn't you want words that move at the speed of life?

You're probably familiar with the *to be* verbs: *is are am was* and *were*. These are passive words, and sometimes they have their place. Sometimes you want to say "The sky was a blue dome overhead" and be done with it.

But at other times we pull out the passive verbs when other perfectly active and visual words are within arm's reach.

If I write *the cat was on the table*, what do you see the cat doing as the sentence plays out in your mind? You're not really sure, are you, because the verb *was* is a wimpy little verb that doesn't pull much weight. If you do a search/replace and replace every *was* with *WAS*, you'll be able to go through your manuscript and replace every wimpy *was* with a hunky anything else.

You could write:

The cat yawned on the table
The cat reclined on the table
The cat retched on the table
The cat curled itself on the table
The cat lay on the table
The cat died on the table
The cat stretched on the table
. . . the possibilities are endless.

I always search for *was* and *were* in every draft and replace them with capitals because I want to see if I can find something better. Sometimes I stick with the simple *was*. Most of the time I find a better, more active way to write my sentence.

If I'm writing in present tense, of course, I search for *am* and *is* as well. I won't replace every active verb, but at least I consider its replacement. That consideration is what teaches us to write tighter.

Weak Adjectives and Enabling Adverbs

An adverb, almost by definition, is employed to support a verb that isn't doing its job. So be brave and search for ly[space], replace it with LY[space], and you should corral a small herd of shifty adverbs. For each of them, either see if you can replace the weak verb with something stronger, or simply cut the adverb. You'll earn a stack of quarters and do your manuscript a big favor.

Someone once reminded me that Jesus taught people by using nouns and strong verbs . . . and we all know how long people have been repeating *his* stories.

Cut the Obvious
True story: on at least two occasions I have taken novels that had gone out of print and sold them to another publisher. But before I handed in the old manuscript to a new publisher, I asked if I could edit them again. Why? "Because," I told one of my editors, "I write tighter now, and I want to improve it."

On those two occasions, I took the manuscript and without deleting a single line of the plot, I cut over nine thousand words from the book. How? By cutting out statements of the obvious like She stood ~~from her chair.~~ Three words, three quarters.

He clapped ~~his hands.~~ (What else is he going to clap, unless he's a walrus?)

They ~~all~~ stood ~~to their feet.~~ (Ditto. Unless they stand on something else, lose the unnecessary words.)

She nodded ~~her head in agreement.~~ (A nod means agreement.)

He stood ~~up.~~ She crouched ~~down.~~ (You can almost always get rid of *up* and *down.*)

She scratched her head ~~with her hand.~~ (Unless she's using her ballpoint pen to take care of the itch.)

She ~~reached out and~~ accepted the trophy.

Do you see how quickly those unnecessary words can add up? So spare a few trees and develop a sense for seeing extraneous verbiage. Then cut, cut, cut.

The Thing about That
I overuse *that* all the time. It slips into my language, my thoughts, and my writing. So whenever I start to cull the weasel words, I do a search for *that*, replace it with THAT, and then carefully consider every THAT I come across. I don't know a test for it except to read the sentence without it—if the sentence makes sense without the THAT, I take it out. If the sentence seems to be missing something important, I leave the *that.* Very simple.

Miscellaneous Weasel Words
Other weasels on almost every list of overused words are *just, very, rather, began to, started to, some, "of the," "there was,"* and *suddenly.*

Just is used too much. You may want to leave it in dialogue, because people do use it in casual conversation, but in nonfiction writing or narrative, you'll probably want to omit *just*. Or replace it with *simply* where applicable.

Very often comes off as amateurish unless it's in a character's dialogue. Remember—the more concise the writing, the stronger the writing, so your sentence will probably be stronger without words like *very*.

Why write *he began to run* or *he started to eat*, when you could write *he ran* or *he ate?* Unless you purposely want someone to be in the process of beginning an activity, the simple past tense will do. But if you want to write:

As he began to eat, a shot rang out, shattering his pasta bowl,

Then *began to* is best.

"Of the" is often used in format titles (The Sword of the Lord and of Gideon), but if you find yourself writing *he hid inside the cloak of the knight*, then ditch the *of the* and write *he hid inside the knight's cloak*. Much, much cleaner.

"There was" is a passive verb linked to a nothing word. So if you find those constructions in your book and you didn't write it for a purposeful reason, cut the nothing words and figure out what you're trying to say. Instead of

There was a peaceful haze over the valley . . .

write

A peaceful haze hovered over the valley.

Suddenly: In fiction, if you are writing and a shot rings out, to your characters it has rung out *suddenly* whether you use the word or not. See for yourself:

> She bent to breathe in the scent of the sweet flowers. "Thank you for the lovely bouquet," she told the little girl. She pressed a kiss to the child's forehead and slipped her fingers around the beribboned stems, ready to hand the flowers to her waiting attendant—

A shot rang out.

She turned, saw horror on her attendant's face, and felt a dull pressure in her back, but that had to be the result of walking all day, from bending to receive dozens of little bouquets, from kissing children and shaking hands and smiling until her jaws ached like they ached now, but no, the pain as lower, but it wasn't pain exactly, it was pressure, and then she heard a splatting sound and felt some thing splash her shoes, probably the children, maybe a child had spilled a bottle of water, but as she looked down she saw that the water was red, as red as her dress, as red as the single rose the prince had left on her pillow this morning—

Sorry—I got a little carried away.

Do you see how you don't need *suddenly* to write a sudden action? If it occurs unexpectedly, it will *feel* sudden.

And I wrote that run-on sentence-paragraph to illustrate something about story time. As a writer, you are the one who controls the passage of time in your story. You can press years into a single sentence—*Years passed, and time did not heal all wounds*—or you can take a single moment, even a second, a draw it out for effect. This is a handy trick if you are writing a car crash, someone being shot or wounded, or the moment when your protagonist receives the shock of bad news.

If you've experienced a moment of tragedy, you can probably remember how it felt: time slowed down, giving you time to record every thought and notice the oddest details. To create the same experience on the written page, write the scene and don't stop the momentum by inserting a period. I wouldn't drag a moment out forever, but you can definitely make time slow to a crawl during dramatic moments. Simply feel free to ignore everything you ever learned in English class and glory in the run-on sentence.

Your Own Personal Weasel Words

Earlier, I told you about the editor pointed out my overuse of the word *pull*. We all have our own personal weasel words, and you may go through phases where you use certain words more than others.

Be especially aware of the body language signals you write—I tend to overuse brows, and sometimes I find eyebrow calisthenics on my pages. Brows are wrinkling, slanting, knitting, lifting, arching, twisting, and lowering. So whether you have a tendency to overuse smiles, shrugs, brows, noses, or whatever, be aware of it. Try to limit yourself to one or two of those expressions per chapter. Or at least per page.

What I Learned From Sol Stein

One of the most useful writing tips I learned from Sol Stein (I highly recommend his books *Stein on Writing* and *How to Grow a Novel*), was this:

$$1 + 1 = 1/2$$
$$1 + 1 + 1 = 1/3$$

That's not the math you learned in school, but it works well in writing. What Stein is warning us about is overwriting, saying the same thing again and again, using different words to repeat ourselves.

Like I did in that last sentence.

I usually fall prey to this tendency when I'm on a roll and the writing is going well. I'm in the groove, the words are flying from my fingertips, and I'm letting it all come out. Problem is, the stuff coming out is the same thought translated into different words.

> He felt angry and frustrated, boiling mad, as frustrated as a dog in a room full of fire hydrants.

When you find that you've piling on layers of the same idea or emotion, choose the best phrase and cut the others. Trust your reader—he'll get it the first time.

Exclamation Points

Unless a character's house is on fire or he's running for his life, you will probably want to lose them. Too many exclamation points come across as amateurish—as though you're working too hard to convey an emotion or sense of urgency. So reserve them for truly dire circumstances, if you use them at all.

Find more elegant ways to convey emotion or urgency through dialogue, interior monologue, or action. And remember—sometimes an emotion is stronger if it's understated. Quiet can be intense.

Scene: Sherry's six-year-old daughter is missing when Sherry tries to pick her up from school.

> Somehow Sherry found herself in the school office, where what seemed like dozens of people offered her a seat, a glass of water, a telephone. Why wouldn't they offer something useful?!
>
> The principal, Mrs. Jones, hurried into the room, breathing hard. "I've just spoken to your daughter's teacher," she said, planting her arm on the tall counter. "And she says a man picked your daughter up ten minutes ago. She assumed he was your husband."
>
> "My husband is dead!" Sherry heard the words rip from her own throat. "And Lily wouldn't go with anybody because I've taught her about stranger danger. Someone has taken her! She's been kidnapped!"
>
> "Calm down, I'm sure there's a logical explanation—"
>
> "You don't know what you're talking about!" Sherry turned and ran from the office in a blind panic.

That's certainly one approach—and one where exclamation marks could be justified. But take a moment to consider the opposite tack:

> Somehow Sherry found herself in the school office, where what seemed like dozens of people offered her a seat, a glass of water, a telephone. Why wouldn't they offer something useful? Why wouldn't one of them calmly step forward and explain where Lily was, and how there'd been a simple misunderstanding—
>
> The principal, Mrs. Jones, hurried into the

room, breathing hard. "I've just spoken to your daughter's teacher—"

"Lily," Sherry said, her voice muffled by the pounding of blood in her ears. "Her name is Lily."

"Of course it is." Mrs. Jones made an effort to smile. "The teacher says a man picked Lily up ten minutes ago. She assumed he was your husband."

Her husband? Sherry stared at the principal as the room shifted and her pulse quickened. "My husband—" her voice faltered—"my husband died four years ago. In Afghanistan."

"I'm so sorry." The principal pressed her hand to her ample chest. "Let me get you a telephone and a place to sit. I'm sure you want to call around and see if Lily could have gone home with one of her friends—"

Sherry cut her off with an uplifted hand. "I have a phone. And I'm going to call the police."

You may disagree, but I find the second scene much more powerful—and the scene doesn't have a single exclamation point.

Other Punctuation Problems: Em Dashes and Ellipses

Some of my writing students probably think I'm being way too picky when I bring up em dashes and ellipses, but I've read enough beginners' manuscripts to know that this area ought to be addressed. If you want your manuscript to rise above the average submission in the slush pile, you should learn to use these punctuation marks properly.

First, know what they are. An em dash is a long hyphen. If you type two hyphens in most word processing programs, the auto correct will automatically insert an em dash (unless that feature has been turned off).

You use em dashes in a couple of ways. First, you can use an em dash to insert a parenthetical phrase.

All manuscripts—including this one—need to be proofread. Just be sure to use an em dash at the beginning and the end of the inserted phrase. Lots of writers make the mistake of using an em dash at the beginning, and a comma where the second em dash should go.

Another use for an em dash, particularly in fiction, is to indicate when someone has been interrupted.

> "Let me tell you a story," Grandpa said, settling back in his chair. "It all began when your grandma was out to get a hog. She had no sooner—"
>
> "Come and eat," Grandma called from the kitchen. "Last one in has to hear the end of that silly story."

In nonfiction, an ellipsis (. . .) is used to indicate the omission of a word or phrase, line or paragraph, from within a quoted text. Four dots are used at the end of a quote to indicate that the original quote continued.

In fiction, an ellipsis is the three dots you often see in dialogue or narrative. Three dots—no period—are used at the end of a sentence in dialogue when a character is trailing off in thought.

> "Seems like only yesterday I was sixteen and dreaming of my first ball gown . . ."

Three dots within a passage of dialogue can be used to indicate a pause in the character's words. This is useful if you want to slow down the reader and add a dreamy quality to the character's speech:

> "Seems like only yesterday I was dreaming of my first ball gown . . . of course that was before my daddy decided no daughter of his would ever take up dancin'."

Sophisticated Sentence Structure

In general, I can think of three principles that will guide you as you construct or revise sentences. Writing a sentence may seem like the easiest thing in the world, but when you begin to wrestle with sentences that contain three or four clauses, getting the structure right can be tricky.

The Pencil Principle: if you consider that a pencil has three parts—the tip, the eraser, and the middle, you can order them by priority: the tip is the most important, the eraser is the second most important, and the middle belongs in last place (though it would be hard to use a pencil without one).

Similarly, the most important segment of your sentence belongs at the end, like the pencil tip. The second most important belongs at the beginning, with the eraser, and the least important can go in the middle.

Example: In one of my books I found myself juggling these three elements:

My angel
Fed acid
To Ramirez.

If I wanted to stress that my angel fed Ramirez *acid*, I'd use my angel first, acid last.

If I wanted to stress that my angel fed acid to *Ramirez*, of all people, I'd use my angel first, Ramirez last.

If I wanted to stress that poor Ramirez ate acid from my *angel*, I'd use Ramirez first, my angel last.

Another principle to keep in mind when you're considering sentence structure is feeling-action-speech order, or the FAS principle. Suppose you want to work with these three elements:

"Get out of here!"
He slammed his fist on the desk.
Anger rose within him.

Which works best for you?

1.) "Get out of here!" He slammed his fist on the desk. Anger rose within him.

2.) Anger rose within him. He slammed his fist on the desk. "Get out of here!"

3.) He slammed his fist on the desk. "Get out of here!" Anger rose within him.

Feeling, action, and then speech, as in example two—will usually work best. In fact, if the emotion is evident in the action, you can save yourself a few quarters and cut the emotional line. Or combine them. Your choice.

> He slammed his fist on the desk ~~as anger rose within him~~. "Get out of here!"

Yet another principle of sentence structure to consider is what I call "the –ing thing." Because writers like to vary their sentence structure, instead of writing:

> Noun verb subject. Noun verb subject. Noun verb subject.
> Bill ate the hamburger. It tasted good. Bill loved his burger.

Sometimes they will write:

> Verbing, noun subject.
> Loving his burger, Bill ate all of it.

The problem arises when writers automatically change the structure without thinking about what they've written:

Smiling, Tom accepted Brenda's invitation is a perfectly good sentence.

Slamming the door behind him, Tom stomped toward the gas station is not. The –ing phrase implies continuous action, and Tom can't be slamming the door behind him while he's stomping toward the gas station. This needs to be changed to:

> After slamming the door, Tom stomped toward the gas station

> OR
> Tom slammed the door, then stomped toward the gas station.

So do a search for your –ing phrases. If they begin a sentence, make sure your active character can do the actions of both phrases simultaneously.

Dialogue Do's and Don'ts

In middle and high school, our English teachers rejoiced when we got jiggy with colorful speech attributes. We had characters chortling, laughing, chuffing, retorting, explaining, bellowing, and burping responses to one another. And our teachers smiled and gave us good grades for our creativity.

If you try the same thing in professional writing, your work will be returned to you faster than a blink. When you write dialogue, whether in fiction or nonfiction, your best bet is to use the word *said* in speaker attributions. Better yet, don't use anything at all, but indicate who's speaking by body movement.

Let's look at a bit that could be part of a nonfiction interview:

> I met up with the two cupcake bakers at their shop on East Avenue. Martha wore a blue apron, Bettye wore pink.
>
> "I always did like girly things," Bettye said, wiping the counter with practiced ease. "Martha's always liked blue."
>
> Martha swiped a stray hank of hair out of her eyes. "I'm not a tomboy; don't you write that. I just like the sea, that's all. It seems cool, and it can get awful hot when you're standin' next to an oven."

In the first paragraph, I used the word *said* and it probably slid right by without stirring even a ripple of recognition in your mind. *Said* is like the word *the*—it's almost invisible when we're reading.

In the third paragraph, it's clear from the physical action (Martha swiping hair out of her face) that this is going to be a Martha paragraph, so any dialogue that follows will come from her. No speaker attribution is needed.

When you're writing dialogue—whether it's in a polished professional article or in the funkiest fiction—try to avoid people growling, giggling, or gasping in their speaker attributions.

Dialogue Explanations

Another situation to avoid whenever possible is dialogue that contains explanations. Like this: "What's wrong?" she asked, confused.

The woman's confusion should be evident in *what she said*, not in the writer's clumsy way of *telling* us she is confused. Remember the old adage *show, don't tell?* This may be brief telling, but it's still telling.

If you really want to add a bit more to emphasize her confusion, do it with description, not a speaker attribution.

> Her eyes clouded as she looked from Tom to Mary. "What's wrong? What aren't you telling me?"

Make sure the confusion is evident in the description and in the dialogue itself.

Dialogue Adverbs

We've already talked about adverbs, and as weak as they are, they're even weaker in speech attributions.

In an early draft of a novel, I once wrote:

> "No slave holder is ever going to sit at my table," Mrs. Haynes said emphatically.

Okay, all is forgivable in a first draft. Writing is revising; we know that. So we get rid of the adverbs after *said.*
Said emphatically. Said angrily. Said softly. Said impetuously.
I could fill a page with said + adverbs, and they'd all be awful. Why spend two quarters when you can keep one? Instead of *said softly*, write *whispered.*
Said angrily? Yelled. (And a note of caution here—we don't want to go too overboard, lest we get into people screaming, roaring, screeching . . . you get the picture.)
Sometimes it's better to spend a few quarters to evoke a visual image: *"I hate her," she said, her upper lip curling.*
As to my example, I ended up writing:

> "No slave holder is ever going to sit at my table." Mrs. Haynes unfolded her napkin with an emphatic snap. "You can be assured of that."

Yes, it's more words, but I traded an adverb for a sensory detail—the snap of the napkin—and that's a trade well made.

Listen to Your Dialogue

I always encourage writers to listen to their dialogue as the computer reads is aloud. In hearing it, you will notice things you might not have noticed as you read it on the page.

(If you work on a Mac, speech capability is built in. If you work on a PC, you can download the free Adobe Reader and use it to have the computer read your manuscript aloud.)

First, does it sound like natural speech? Do your speakers use contractions, run-on sentences, and contradict each other? Real people do. And while it's true that dialogue is not exact speech, but an *approximation* of real speech, a lot of beginners' dialogue is neither.

Writers often drop character names into dialogue to help clarify things for the reader, but how often do you actually say the name of the person you're talking to? Not often, I'd bet. So delete names in your dialogue if they seem superfluous.

Look at this exchange:

> "Hi, Bob. How are you?"
>
> "Just fine, thanks. And you? How're the wife and kids?"
>
> "Well, Marge had the flu, as you know, and little Billy needs braces. Plus we just found out the roof leaks, so we will be needing to raid the savings account again. Seems like we just can't get ahead."
>
> "Well, it's nothing to be ashamed of. Everyone goes through tight spots. Now I've got to run. I'll see you later."
>
> "Okay. Nice seeing you."
>
> "Nice seeing you, too."

Snooze-a-rama! Heaven help us if all books were written as badly as that.

First, see all those routine greetings? The "how are you"s and "See you laters?" Get rid of them; they're accomplishing nothing.

You could just as easily write:

> Bob and Tom met at the corner. After greeting
> Tom, Bob looked his friend directly in the eye and
> asked if they were having financial difficulties.
> "Why would you ask that?"
> Bob shrugged. "It's nothing to be ashamed of.
> Everyone goes through tight spots."

See what I mean? Cut to the chase every time. Those little pleasantries mean nothing—unless they're highly unusual and you want the reader to notice how stilted someone is during the usual pleasantries.

Second, watch out for the "as you know, Bob"s that often occur in beginning novelists' dialogue. Do not have your characters telling each other things they already know. Nothing more obviously shows the writer at work than exposition planted in a conversation.

If you need to get exposition into dialogue so your reader will know what's going on, one of the most common ways is to have someone new come to town. This new person wouldn't know the town history or what happened to a particular character, so a native can show the newbie around and fill him in. You see this tactic employed all the time in books and films, and it works well.

I remember watching one of the muppet movies—I forget which—and Kermit the Frog was talking to actress Diana Rigg. She was relating the long and convoluted history of other characters when he interrupted: "Excuse me—why are you telling me all this?"

She lifted one shoulder in an elegant shrug. "It's exposition. It has to go *somewhere*."

And away they went.

Don't be so obvious. Do your best to find a creative way to impart information your reader needs to know.

Third, listen to the computer read your dialogue because the computer will not add emotion the way your mind will when you read it. The computer's slightly robotic voice can be a benefit if it reveals where your dialogue lacks emotional depth.

Free tip: one way to show that a character's native language is *not* English is to eliminate all the contractions from his dialogue.

The dialogue then becomes stiff and stilted, just as it would if the character were just learning English.

Do not remove contractions from the dialogue of *all* your characters or they'll all sound stiff!

No Ping Pong Allowed

If you look carefully at your dialogue, you may find that you are writing "on the nose"—with no subtlety or subtext. And that for every conversational "ping," the other character answers with an appropriate "pong."

Real conversation isn't like that . . . unless it's deadly boring.

Consider this exchange:

> Tom carried the bag of groceries into the kitchen where Brenda waited.
> "Did you get the catsup?" she asked without looking up.
> "Yes, I did. Heinz. Because I know you like it."
> "I like any kind. As long as it's on sale."
> "Well, this one wasn't."
> "On sale?"
> "Right. But the mustard was twenty cents off. And by the way, I saw Melissa standing over in produce."
> "Melissa?" Brenda finally looked up. "Did she speak?"
> "Sure she did. She said hi and I said hi and then she asked if I'd seen Toby."
> "Well?"
> "I hadn't seen Toby."
> "Did you tell her that?"
> "Well, she asked, didn't she?"

ZZZzzzzzzzz. Let's try again.

> Tom carried the groceries into the kitchen where Brenda waited.
> "Catsup?" she asked without looking up.
> "Heinz. Because you won't eat anything else."
> "I like any kind, as long as it's on sale."

"I saw Melissa standing over in produce."

"Was it?" She turned, finally. "Was the catsup on sale?"

"Did you hear me? I saw Melissa." He bent closer to look into her eyes. "She asked if I'd seen Toby."

Brenda blinked. "You must think I'm some kind of tightwad."

Tom slammed his fist onto the counter. "Good grief, Brenda, how long are you going to ignore that missing kid?"

Ah . . . much better. The first passage is an exercise in tedium; the second crackles with suspense. There are undercurrents and questions are flying through the reader's mind. Why is Brenda so concerned about the cost of catsup? Who's Melissa, and why doesn't Brenda want to hear about her? Why is Tom so upset? And who in the heck is Toby?

(I don't know the answers to any of those questions. If you do, feel free to finish the story.)

Don't let your dialogue click back and forth like a metronome. Keep it off-balance, and you'll keep your characters off-balance. Keep your characters off-balance and you'll keep your readers off-balance. And that's a good thing because it add suspense to any novel.

Don't write dialogue phonetically.

Years ago writers would approximate the sound of spoken speech by writing dialogue the way it sounded. Who can forget Mammy's speech in *Gone With the Wind*?

"Ef you doan care 'bout how folks talks 'bout dis fambly, Ah does," she rumbled. "Ah ain' gwine stand by an' have eve'body at de pahty sayin' how you ain' fotched up right. Ah has tole you an' tole you dat you kin allus tell a lady by dat she eat lak a bird. An' Ah ain' aimin' ter have you go ter Mist' Wilkes' an' eat lak a fe'el han' an' gobble lak a hawg."[3]

We don't write dialogue phonetically anymore for several reasons: it's hard to read, it breaks the fictive dream, and it's not politically correct. It's fine to drop a 'g' occasionally, or change *got* to to *gotta*, especially if it results in a more natural speech for your character, but please resist the urge to spell things the way they sound.

If you want to signify that a character is from a different country, read some books written in that country and get a feel for the way the natives use language. For instance, I wrote a series of books in Ireland and spent some time there doing research. I kept a little notebook and would jot down little phrases I heard people use in ordinary conversation. I also copied down unique road signs because they gave me additional colorful vocabulary. (For instance, on the side of a rocky hill in the U.S. you'd see a sign saying "Watch for falling rocks." In Ireland, in the same situation I saw, "Mind your windscreen."

In her novel *The Help*, Kathryn Stockett did an amazing job of creating the sound and rhythm of southern black speech with word choice. Here's a paragraph from the first chapter:

> By the time she a year old, Mae Mobley following me around everywhere I go. Five o'clock would come round and she'd be hanging on my Dr. Scholl shoe, dragging over the floor, crying like I weren't never coming back. Miss Leefolt, she'd narrow up her eyes at me like I done something wrong, unhitch that crying baby off my foot. I reckon that's the risk you run, letting somebody else raise you chilluns.[4]

By sprinkling your character's conversation with unique phrases—whether picked up in another country, another profession, or another social group—you will singularize your characters. Soon your readers will know which character is speaking by the words he uses . . . or so we hope. Creating particular and unique characters is one of our goal as writers.

Be Kind to Yourself and Avoid Dinnertime Dialogue
I'm not saying that you should never write a scene where people talk and eat at the same time. I was merely searching for a way to

describe a difficult situation to write. I stumbled into it once, and I'll never do it again.

In my novel *The Canopy*, I wrote a scene where ten characters sat around a dinner table and discussed their expedition into the jungle. Not only where there ten people, but they were from different countries—a Russian, an Englishman, a couple of Americans, a Peruvian, a Frenchman, and others I've forgotten. Because it would have been beyond awful to end every bit of dialogue with "so-and-so said," I resorted to bits of body language to make it clear who was speaking. So characters were casting looks, passing plantains, shrugging, dropping spoons, picking up spoons, waving forks, dropping napkins, picking up napkins—well, you get the picture.

To make matters worse, my friend Bill Myers and I recorded the book for audio, using accents for each of the characters. Bill read all the male POV scenes and dialogue, and I read all the female scenes and dialogue. But when we got to the dinner table scene, with all the characters talking at once, I think Bill was tempted to bash me over the head with the manuscript. Talk about a challenge!

So do yourself a favor—if at all possible limit conversations in your book to two or three people at a time. You'll be glad you did. Besides, when you're at a banquet, who do you really talk to? The people on either side of you, right? So it is natural to keep dialogue between a few.

One day you'll thank me for that little tip.

Interior Monologue

I spent a lot of time on this in *Lessons from the Writing Front: Point of View*, but I'll review it here because it's an important part of getting your manuscript ready for submission.

When you are using a limited point of view—one POV per scene—the things you write are limited to what your POV character sees, hears, tastes, touches, senses, knows, and feels. So if he thinks *I want to get out of here*, you do not need to write *he thought* afterward. Neither do you need to place his thoughts in italics.

Because you're in limited third person, the things you're writing come from his head, so the reader intuits that the thoughts come from the character's consciousness. You don't need to remind him. You don't need to write *he thought*, *he mused*, *or he recollected*. You don't need to put it in quotes (they're only for spoken speech) or in bold. You simply write it.

> Johnson walked into the room he'd left ten years before. No one had disturbed the furniture as far as he could tell, but the upholstery looked faded from the sun. Right over there, on that row of tile in front of the fireplace, Lydia had looked him in the eye and said she loved him. Really loved him. And she meant it—he read sincerity in her eyes and in the curve of her mouth. But then she walked away, looking for her rich third cousin, and then she'd married him, despite Johnson's pleas.
>
> What a fraud.

Poor guy. He walks into a room and we see what he sees because we're looking through his eyes. We then access his memories, of a day ten years earlier when Lydia had told him she loved him and then ran after some rich guy. And then we hear, straight from Johnson's brain, what he thinks of the lady: what a fraud. (I know, John's thought is pretty tame. But what can I say? He's a laid back kind of guy.)

So spare yourself some quarters and cut all the "he thoughts" if they are signaling interior monologue. If you find a "he wondered," you can usually turn the sentence into a question.

From:

He wondered if she had ever loved him.

to

Had she ever loved him?

If you ever have characters mumbling under their breaths because you're really trying to slip the reader some information, please change it to interior monologue instead--unless your character is drunk or suffering from a mental illness.

If you have pages and pages of interior monologue, you

probably need to take some of it out and turn it into a scene. If your character drifts back in time for more than a page or so, you'd probably be better off if you lift out that memory and turn it into a full-fledged flashback, a separate scene . . . and then insert it only when (and not a moment before) the reader needs to know that information. If the reader doesn't need to know the information, place it in your "cut materials" folder. Where it can wait. And rest in peace.

Two Hads Will Do It

One final foolproof way for novelists to spruce up their scenes and earn a few quarters.

A *flashback* is a full scene that takes place before the present story time. A *recollection* is a little snippet that takes place within a present time scene. The scene I created earlier about Johnson and Lydia contained a brief recollection.

> Johnson walked into the room he'd left ten years before. No one had disturbed the furniture as far as he could tell, but the upholstery looked faded from the sun. Right over there, on that row of tile in front of the fireplace, Lydia **had** looked him in the eye and said she loved him. Really loved him. And she meant it—he read sincerity in her eyes and in the curve of her mouth. But then she walked away, looking for her rich third cousin, and then she **had** married him, despite Johnson's pleas.
>
> What a fraud.

What I want you to notice are the two *hads*. The first is the key that takes us back to the day when Lydia looked him in the eye . . . and the second, pertaining to Lydia's marrying her cousin, brings us back to present story time.

You do not need *hads* any where else in the recollection. Novice writers might have written:

> . . . Lydia **had** looked him in the eye and said she loved him. Really loved him. And she **had** meant it—he **had** read sincerity in her eyes and in

the curve of her mouth. But then she **had** walked away, looking for her third rich cousin, and then she **had** married him . . .

When inserting a recollection, remember that the first *had* takes you back, the second brings you forward. Simple and elegant. A flash back can work the same way, depending on how it's structured. You could indicate the start of a flashback by inserting the date in front of the scene:

> January 3, 1517.
> The wind blew steadily at the mouth of the cave, pushing the men back.

In this case you don't need any *hads* at all, because the date tells the reader that this scene took place before the present story time (assuming that present story time is after January 1517).

Or you could write the scene and use a *had* to take the reader back and another to bring her forward:

> She **had** turned ten that month, and remembered little about her party except that Uncle Jack brought a bouquet of red balloons . . .
> . . .
> But she **had** been a child then, and now she was a woman grown. And now 'twas time to put away childish things.

In Summation

Self-editing is an art, but revision is necessary. I write my novels in at least five drafts, and I never feel that they are 100 percent perfect. My friend novelist Alton Gansky once reminded me that if a novel is 100,000 words and 99.9 percent perfect, it still contains 100 errors.

What makes revision even more challenging is that we're not searching for concrete "errors" like typos. We are looking for ways to make language clearer, to amplify the art, to ratchet up the emotional experience, and solidify a theme. We are working to focus the total effect of our work, and sometimes we are only guessing at what is best.

So I hope these few guidelines, pointers, and tips have been helpful as you set about revising your work. I will leave you with two additional thoughts:

If you find a section of your book isn't working—if it isn't deepening character or advancing plot in fiction, or if it isn't providing more information or motivating your reader in nonfiction--you need to place it in your "cut materials" file and leave it there for several days. If you forget about it, it probably wasn't supposed to be included in your book.

And always remember that writing is a craft and an art. The more you learn, the more you realize you need to learn, and that's what makes writing so amazing and challenging.

So go ahead—get back to work on your manuscript and make it the best it can be. We're waiting to see what you do with it.

Thank you for purchasing this book in **Writing Lessons from the Front.** If you find any typos in this book, please write and let us know: hunthaven@gmail.com.

We would also appreciate it if you would be kind enough to leave a review of this book on Amazon. Thank you!

Writing Lessons from the Front:

1. **The Plot Skeleton**
2. **Creating Extraordinary Characters**
3. **Point of View**
4. **Tracking Down the Weasel Words**
5. **Evoking Emotion**
6. **Write Your Book: Process and Planning**

ABOUT THE AUTHOR

Angela Hunt writes for readers who have learned to expect the unexpected from this versatile writer. With over four million copies of her books sold worldwide, she is the best-selling author of more than 120 works ranging from picture books (*The Tale of Three Trees*) to novels and nonfiction.

Now that her two children have reached their twenties, Angie and her husband live in Florida with Very Big Dogs (a direct result of watching *Turner and Hooch* too many times). This affinity for mastiffs has not been without its rewards—one of their dogs was featured on *Live with Regis and Kelly* as the second-largest canine in America. Their dog received this dubious honor after an all-expenses-paid trip to Manhattan for the dog and the Hunts, complete with VIP air travel and a stretch limo in which they toured New York City. Afterward, the dog gave out pawtographs at the airport.

Angela admits to being fascinated by animals, medicine, unexplained phenomena, and "just about everything." Books, she says, have always shaped her life— in the fifth grade she learned how to flirt from reading *Gone with the Wind*.

Her books have won the coveted Christy Award, several Angel Awards from Excellence in Media, and the Gold and Silver Medallions from *Foreword Magazine*'s Book of the Year Award. In 2007, her novel *The Note* was featured as a Christmas movie on the Hallmark channel. She recently completed her doctorate in biblical literature and is now finishing her doctorate in Theology.

When she's not home writing, Angie often travels to teach writing workshops at schools and writers' conferences. And to talk about her dogs, of course. Readers may visit her web site at www.angelahuntbooks.com.

Selected Books by Angela Hunt

The Offering
The Fine Art of Insincerity
Five Miles South of Peculiar
The Face
Let Darkness Come
The Elevator
The Novelist
The Awakening
The Truth Teller
Unspoken
Uncharted
The Justice
The Canopy
The Immortal
Doesn't She Look Natural?
She Always Wore Red
She's In a Better Place
The Pearl
The Note
The Debt
Then Comes Marriage
The Shadow Women
Dreamers
Brothers
Journey
Roanoke
Jamestown
Hartford
Rehoboth
Charles Towne
The Proposal
The Silver Sword
The Golden Cross
The Velvet Shadow
The Emerald Isle

ENDNOTES

[1]Jodi Picoult, *Second Glance* (New York: Washington Square Press, 2008).
[2]Angela Hunt, *Magdalene* (Wheaton, IL: Tyndale House Publishers, 2006).
[3]Margaret Mitchell, *Gone With the Wind* (New York: MacMillan Company, 1936), p. 54.
[4]Kathryn Stockett, *The Help* (New York: Berkley Trade, 2011).

3674874R00022

Made in the USA
San Bernardino, CA
15 August 2013